Unseen Potential:
The Art and Science of Doing Great Things

Manuel Henninger

Table Of Contents

Introduction

In a world filled with endless possibilities, there exists within each of us a reservoir of untapped potential, waiting to be discovered, nurtured, and harnessed. This potential is the key to unlocking the extraordinary, and it's the driving force behind our quest to accomplish great things. Welcome to "Unseen Potential: The Art and Science of Doing Great Things."

We live in an era where the boundaries of human achievement are constantly pushed, where individuals and groups are rewriting the rules of what's possible. Whether it's in the realm of science, technology, business, arts, or personal development, there's a shared understanding that greatness is attainable, but often hidden beneath the surface.

This book is a comprehensive exploration of the hidden potential that resides within each of us. It is a journey into the art and science of realizing our aspirations, ambitions, and dreams. Together, we'll embark on a transformative expedition, armed with knowledge, inspiration, and actionable strategies that will help you uncover your dormant talents, overcome challenges, and embrace the path to greatness.

In the chapters that follow, we will delve into the secrets of understanding yourself better, identifying your unique strengths, and tapping into the profound wisdom of human potential. We'll explore the scientific principles that underpin success, from the psychology of achievement to the neuroscience of peak performance. We'll discuss the critical importance of mindset, the fuel that propels you forward or holds you back, and how to cultivate the resilience necessary to persevere in the face of adversity.

We'll journey through the terrain of goal setting, where we'll discover the power of setting ambitious, yet achievable objectives, and the strategies to turn dreams into reality. Passion and purpose will become our guiding stars as we explore the profound significance of aligning your actions with your inner calling and values.

"Unseen Potential" is more than just a book; it's your personal guide to transformation. Whether you're aspiring to reach new heights in your career, make a meaningful impact on your community, or simply lead a life filled with fulfillment and purpose, the principles within these pages will serve as your compass.

Together, we'll unveil the greatness that resides within you, hidden but waiting to be awakened. It's time to embark on this extraordinary journey of self-discovery, empowerment, and achievement. The adventure begins now.

Chapter 1

Mindset Mastery

In the ever-evolving landscape of personal and professional development, the concept of a "growth mindset" has gained significant attention and recognition. Coined by psychologist Carol Dweck, the growth mindset is a simple yet profound idea that can transform lives. It's the belief that abilities and intelligence can be developed through dedication, hard work, and perseverance. In this article, we will explore the power of a growth mindset and how it can unlock new opportunities and success in various aspects of life.

The Foundation of a Growth Mindset:
At the heart of a growth mindset is the understanding that challenges, setbacks, and failures are not roadblocks but stepping stones on the path to improvement. Those who embrace a growth mindset see effort as

the path to mastery and view criticism as valuable feedback. They believe in the potential for change and that their abilities are not fixed traits but can be developed over time.

1. Embracing Challenges:
Individuals with a growth mindset welcome challenges as opportunities for growth. Instead of avoiding difficult tasks, they approach them with enthusiasm. They understand that confronting challenges head-on allows them to stretch their abilities and learn new skills. This willingness to tackle challenges is a key driver of personal and professional development.

2. Persistence and Resilience:
A growth mindset encourages resilience in the face of adversity. When setbacks occur, those with a growth mindset don't see them as failures but as temporary obstacles. This mindset fosters a "never give up" attitude,

motivating individuals to persevere through difficulties until they achieve their goals.

3. Learning and Improvement:
Continuous learning is a cornerstone of the growth mindset. Individuals with this mindset actively seek opportunities to acquire new knowledge and skills. They value the process of learning itself and understand that improvement is an ongoing journey. As a result, they are more likely to achieve excellence in their chosen pursuits.

4. Embracing Effort:
In a growth mindset, effort is seen as a path to mastery. Rather than expecting immediate success, individuals are prepared to invest time and energy into their endeavors. They understand that sustained effort and practice are essential for reaching high levels of performance.

5. Overcoming Limiting Beliefs:

A growth mindset helps individuals break free from limiting beliefs about their abilities. It encourages them to challenge the notion that they have fixed limitations and instead fosters a belief in their potential for growth and development.

Application in Various Aspects of Life:
The power of a growth mindset extends across diverse areas of life:

1. Education: Students with a growth mindset tend to excel academically because they approach learning with enthusiasm and resilience.

2. Career: In the professional world, individuals with a growth mindset are more likely to take on challenging projects, adapt to change, and advance in their careers.

3. Relationships: A growth mindset can improve relationships by fostering empathy,

understanding, and a willingness to learn and grow together.

4. Health and Wellness: Embracing a growth mindset in the realm of health and wellness can lead to positive lifestyle changes, improved physical fitness, and better mental health.

In a world that is constantly changing and presenting new challenges, the power of a growth mindset cannot be underestimated. It's a mindset that enables individuals to adapt, grow, and thrive in the face of adversity. By embracing challenges, persisting through difficulties, valuing effort, and believing in the potential for improvement, anyone can harness the transformative power of a growth mindset and unlock new opportunities for success in all aspects of life.

Cultivating a Growth Mindset: Techniques for Personal Life and Success

Success in both our personal and professional lives often hinges on our mindset. While a fixed mindset can limit our potential, a growth mindset can open doors to limitless possibilities. The good news is that cultivating a growth mindset is achievable through deliberate practice and mindset-shifting techniques. In this article, we will explore practical strategies to nurture a growth mindset and apply it to achieve personal growth and success.

1. Embrace Challenges:
One of the fundamental principles of a growth mindset is to welcome challenges as opportunities for learning and growth. Instead of avoiding difficulties, actively seek out tasks that push your boundaries. Understand that facing challenges head-on

can help you acquire new skills and become more resilient.

2. View Failure as Feedback:
Failure is not the end; it's a valuable part of the learning process. When you encounter setbacks, adopt the perspective that they offer valuable feedback. Analyze what went wrong, adjust your approach, and use failure as a stepping stone toward improvement. Remember that even the most successful individuals have faced failures on their path to greatness.

3. Cultivate a Love for Learning:
Continuous learning is at the core of a growth mindset. Develop a curiosity for new ideas and knowledge. Seek out opportunities to acquire new skills, whether through formal education, online courses, or self-directed learning. Embrace the joy of discovering new things, and remember that the process of learning itself is a reward.

4. Develop Resilience:
Resilience is the ability to bounce back from adversity. Cultivating resilience is crucial for personal growth and success. When faced with setbacks, remind yourself that setbacks are temporary. Focus on developing your ability to persevere through challenges and maintain a positive outlook.

5. Replace Negative Self-Talk:
Pay attention to your inner dialogue. Replace self-limiting beliefs with empowering thoughts. Challenge negative self-talk and replace it with affirmations that reinforce your belief in your potential for growth and success. Practice self-compassion and treat yourself with kindness and encouragement.

6. Seek Constructive Feedback:
Feedback, whether positive or negative, is a valuable tool for growth. Actively seek feedback from others, whether it's in your personal relationships or professional life.

Use this feedback as a means to improve and grow. Remember, feedback is not a reflection of your worth but an opportunity for progress.

7. Set Meaningful Goals:
Establish clear and achievable goals that inspire you. Break these goals down into manageable steps. A growth mindset thrives on progress and accomplishment. Celebrate your achievements along the way, and view setbacks as opportunities to refine your approach.

8. Surround Yourself with Positivity:
Your environment plays a significant role in shaping your mindset. Surround yourself with positive influences, supportive friends, mentors, and role models who inspire you to maintain a growth-oriented perspective. Minimize exposure to negativity and self-doubt.

9. Practice Patience:

Cultivating a growth mindset is a journey that takes time. Be patient with yourself and acknowledge that change doesn't happen overnight. Consistently apply these techniques, and over time, you will notice a shift in your mindset and its positive impact on your personal life and success.

A growth mindset is not a fixed trait; it's a skill that can be developed and nurtured throughout life. By actively embracing challenges, viewing failure as feedback, cultivating a love for learning, and practicing resilience, you can unlock your potential for personal growth and success. Remember that the power to change your mindset lies within you, and with dedication and persistence, you can shape a future filled with continuous growth and achievement.

Cultivating a Growth Mindset for Professional Success

In the fast-paced and ever-changing landscape of the professional world, a growth mindset is a powerful asset. This mindset, which centers on the belief that abilities and intelligence can be developed through dedication and hard work, can be a key driver of success. In this article, we'll explore techniques to cultivate a growth mindset in your professional life and leverage it for greater success.

1. Embrace Challenges:
One of the fundamental aspects of a growth mindset is the willingness to embrace challenges. Instead of shying away from difficult tasks or projects, view them as opportunities for growth. Challenge is where learning happens, and by tackling these challenges head-on, you not only expand your skill set but also demonstrate your resilience and determination.

2. Learn from Failures:

A growth mindset encourages you to see failures not as dead-ends but as stepping stones to success. When you encounter setbacks or make mistakes, take the time to reflect on what went wrong and what you can learn from the experience. This introspective approach helps you avoid making the same mistakes in the future and allows for continuous improvement.

3. Seek Feedback:
Feedback is a valuable tool for personal and professional growth. In a growth mindset, feedback is seen as a source of insight and an opportunity for improvement. Seek feedback from colleagues, mentors, and supervisors, and use it to refine your skills and enhance your performance. Don't take criticism personally; instead, view it as a means to evolve and excel.

4. Cultivate a Love for Learning:
Continuous learning is at the core of a growth mindset. Develop a genuine passion

for acquiring new knowledge and skills. Stay curious and open-minded, and actively seek out opportunities for professional development. This might include attending workshops, taking online courses, or simply reading books and articles related to your field.

5. Set Ambitious Goals:

A growth mindset encourages you to set ambitious yet achievable goals. These goals should challenge you and push you out of your comfort zone. By striving for these objectives, you not only stretch your abilities but also foster a sense of purpose and direction in your professional life.

6. Develop Resilience:

Resilience is the ability to bounce back from setbacks and keep moving forward. Cultivate resilience by focusing on solutions rather than dwelling on problems. Maintain a positive attitude and keep your eye on your long-term objectives. Remember that setbacks are temporary, and with determination, you can overcome them.

7. Surround Yourself with Positivity:
Your environment plays a significant role in shaping your mindset. Surround yourself with colleagues, mentors, and friends who support your growth and encourage your aspirations. Avoid toxic or negative influences that can hinder your progress.

8. Visualize Success:
Visualization is a powerful technique to reinforce a growth mindset. Picture yourself achieving your professional goals, envision the steps required to get there, and imagine the sense of accomplishment and fulfillment that comes with success. This mental exercise can boost your confidence and motivation.

Cultivating a growth mindset in your professional life is a journey that requires dedication and commitment. By embracing challenges, learning from failures, seeking feedback, and fostering a love for learning, you can position yourself for continuous growth and success. Remember that a growth mindset is not just about skills; it's about developing the resilience, determination, and adaptability needed to excel in the dynamic world of work. With a growth mindset as your foundation, your professional possibilities are limitless.

Chapter 2

Goal Setting and Achievement

Goals are the compass that guides us through life's journey. Whether big or small, personal or professional, setting meaningful goals is a fundamental aspect of human motivation and achievement. But there's more to goal-setting than meets the eye—it's both an art and a science, a delicate balance between aspiration and strategy. In this exploration, we'll delve into the art and science of setting meaningful goals and discover how this process can transform our lives.

The Art of Goal-Setting

1. Vision and Clarity: The art of setting meaningful goals begins with a clear vision. What do you truly desire? Define your goals with precision, picturing the desired outcome vividly in your mind. This clarity

serves as your North Star, guiding your actions.

2. Passion and Purpose: Meaningful goals are fueled by passion and purpose. They should resonate with your values and ignite a fire within you. When your goals align with your deepest desires, they become more than tasks; they become a calling.

3. Stretching Comfort Zones: Artful goal-setting involves pushing boundaries. Meaningful goals often require you to step out of your comfort zone, to challenge yourself, and to embrace growth. It's in this discomfort that transformation happens.

4. Emotional Connection: Goals should evoke emotions. The art lies in feeling deeply connected to your goals. When your heart is invested, you'll find the motivation to overcome obstacles and stay committed.

The Science of Goal-Setting

1. Specificity: The science of goal-setting emphasizes specificity. Goals must be clear and well-defined. Vague objectives make it challenging to measure progress and stay focused.

2. Measurable: Goals should be quantifiable. Without measurable criteria, it's difficult to track your progress and determine when you've achieved success.

3. Achievable and Realistic: While stretching comfort zones is vital, goals should also be achievable and realistic. Unrealistic goals can lead to frustration and abandonment of your pursuit.

4. Time-Bound: Setting a timeframe is crucial. Without deadlines, goals can languish indefinitely. The science of goal-setting dictates that you set target dates for milestones and the final achievement.

5. Planning and Strategy: Goals require a plan of action. The science lies in breaking down your goals into actionable steps. This roadmap ensures that you know precisely what needs to be done.

The Symbiosis of Art and Science:
Setting meaningful goals is a dance between the art and science. The art fuels your passion and vision, inspiring you to reach for the stars. The science provides structure and strategy, turning your dreams into actionable plans.

Tips for Effective Goal-Setting

1. Write It Down: Putting your goals in writing solidifies your commitment.

2. Review Regularly: Keep your goals in sight. Regularly reviewing them reinforces your dedication.

3. Stay Flexible: Life can throw curveballs. Be open to adapting your goals when necessary.

4. Seek Support: Share your goals with others who can provide encouragement and accountability.

5. Celebrate Milestones: Acknowledge your progress along the way. Celebrating small wins can boost motivation.

In conclusion, the art and science of setting meaningful goals provide the framework for personal and professional growth. By blending your passion, vision, and purpose with specific, measurable, and achievable objectives, you create a powerful roadmap to success. Remember, your goals are not just the destination; they're the journey, the catalyst for self-discovery and transformation. Embrace this process, and you'll find that the pursuit of your dreams is a profoundly enriching adventure.

Accomplishing the Art and Science of Setting Meaningful Goals

Setting meaningful goals is a transformative process that requires a combination of artful inspiration and scientific precision. To successfully accomplish this, consider the following strategies:

1. Self-Reflection and Clarity:
   - Art: Begin with self-reflection. What truly matters to you? What are your passions, values, and long-term aspirations?
   - Science: Be specific about your goals. Define them clearly, making sure they are measurable and achievable. This clarity ensures you know exactly what you're aiming for.

2. Prioritize and Focus:
   - Art: Prioritize your goals based on their personal significance. Focus on those that

align most closely with your values and passions.

- Science: Concentrate your efforts on a limited number of goals at a time. Overcommitting can lead to burnout and reduced effectiveness.

3. Break Down into Actionable Steps:

- Art: Create a vision board or a visual representation of your goals. This artistic process can help you stay connected emotionally to your objectives.

- Science: Break each goal into smaller, manageable tasks. Create a timeline with deadlines for completing these tasks. This step-by-step approach makes your goals actionable.

4. Stay Motivated:

- Art: Continually remind yourself of the emotional reasons behind your goals. Visualize the end result and how it will positively impact your life.

- Science: Establish a system of accountability. Share your goals with a trusted friend, family member, or mentor who can provide support and motivation.

5. Embrace Resilience and Adaptability:
- Art: Understand that setbacks and challenges are part of the journey. Embrace them as opportunities for growth and learning.
- Science: If you encounter obstacles, adjust your plan without losing sight of the end goal. Flexibility is a key scientific strategy for goal achievement.

6. Celebrate Milestones:
- Art: Celebrate your progress along the way. Acknowledge and savor the small victories to maintain enthusiasm.
- Science: Regularly review your goals and assess your progress. Adjust your approach if necessary to ensure you stay on track.

7. Continuous Learning:

- Art: Approach the pursuit of your goals as a learning experience. Embrace curiosity and a growth mindset.

- Science: Seek knowledge and resources relevant to your goals. Learning and adapting are vital scientific components of goal achievement.

8. Stay Organized

- Art: Use creative tools like vision boards, journals, or mind maps to keep your goals visually present.

- Science: Utilize organizational tools, such as calendars, to-do lists, and project management apps, to stay on top of tasks and deadlines.

9. Balance and Well-being:

- Art: Ensure a healthy work-life balance. The art of self-care and well-being is essential for maintaining the motivation and energy required for goal accomplishment.

- Science: Set specific goals related to self-care and well-being, such as exercise, sleep, and stress management, to support your overall progress.

10. Review and Adjust:
   - Art: Reflect regularly on your journey. Assess your personal growth and development as you work towards your goals.
   - Science: Scientifically, adaptability is crucial. If you find your goals evolving or shifting over time, adjust your plan accordingly.

In conclusion, the art and science of setting meaningful goals are complementary forces that, when combined, can propel you toward personal and professional success. By merging emotional connection, inspiration, and vision with specific, measurable, and actionable steps, you create a dynamic approach that maximizes your potential for achieving what truly matters to you. Remember, the journey of goal achievement is a masterpiece in progress, where the canvas of your life transforms with every step you take.

Chapter 3

Self-Discovery

Embarking on a journey of self-discovery is an enriching and transformative experience. It's a path that leads you to uncover your hidden talents, explore your passions, and ultimately, find your purpose in life. Here's a step-by-step guide to help you embark on this exciting journey:

1. Self-Reflection:
   - Start with Silence: Find a quiet space where you can reflect without distractions. Close your eyes, take deep breaths, and clear your mind.

   - Journaling: Begin by writing down your thoughts, feelings, and aspirations. Consider questions like, "What am I truly passionate about?" and "What activities bring me joy and fulfillment?"

2. Explore Your Interests:

- Curiosity as a Compass: Follow your curiosity. Explore hobbies, activities, and subjects that have always piqued your interest, even if they seem unrelated to your current path.

- Experiment: Don't be afraid to try new things. Attend workshops, take up a new sport, or enroll in a class that intrigues you. New experiences can uncover hidden talents.

3. Identify Your Strengths:

- Feedback from Others: Seek input from friends, family, and colleagues about your strengths and unique qualities. Sometimes, others can see things in us that we overlook.

- Self-Assessment: Use personality assessments like the Myers-Briggs Type Indicator (MBTI) or StrengthsFinder to gain insights into your natural strengths and preferences.

4. Reflect on Past Successes:

   - Achievement Journal: Create a journal where you record your past accomplishments and moments of pride. Analyze these experiences to discover patterns and recurring themes.

5. Seek Inspiration:

      - Read Widely: Explore books, biographies, and articles about individuals who have found their passions and purpose. Their stories can provide valuable insights.

   - Mentorship: Find a mentor or coach who can guide you on your journey. Their wisdom and experience can be invaluable in uncovering your talents and purpose.

6. Embrace Challenges:

   - Overcome Fear of Failure: Understand that setbacks and failures are part of the self-discovery process. Embrace them as opportunities for growth.

- Push Boundaries: Challenge yourself to step out of your comfort zone. Personal growth often occurs when you take on new challenges.

7. Practice Mindfulness:
   - Mindful Meditation: Practice mindfulness meditation to become more self-aware and in tune with your thoughts and emotions. This can lead to profound insights.

8. Connect with Your Passions:
   - Passion Projects: Dedicate time to activities that genuinely excite you. The more you engage with your passions, the clearer your purpose may become.

9. Define Your Values:
   - Core Values: Identify your core values. What principles guide your decisions and actions? Your purpose often aligns with your deeply held values.

10. Set Goals with Purpose:

- SMART Goals: Create goals that are Specific, Measurable, Achievable, Relevant, and Time-bound. These goals should reflect your passions and purpose.

11. Embrace Patience:

- Time and Patience: Self-discovery is a lifelong journey. Be patient with yourself and allow the process to unfold naturally.

12. Share Your Gifts:

- Give Back: As you uncover your talents and purpose, find ways to use them to benefit others. Sharing your gifts can provide a profound sense of fulfillment.

13. Regularly Reflect:

- Continuous Reflection: Set aside regular intervals to revisit your journey of self-discovery. Celebrate your progress and make adjustments as needed.

Remember, the journey of self-discovery is deeply personal and unique to each individual. Embrace the process, stay open to new experiences, and trust that, over time, you will uncover your hidden talents, passions, and purpose. Your path to self-discovery is a beautiful and rewarding adventure that can lead to a life filled with meaning and fulfillment.

Peak Performance

High achievers, those who consistently perform at their best, seem to possess a magic formula that eludes the rest of us. But the truth is, their success isn't a result of luck or innate talent alone. It's the product of deliberate habits, routines, and practices that foster excellence. In this article, we'll delve into the world of high achievers to uncover the secrets behind their consistent top performance.

1. Setting Clear Goals and Priorities:

High achievers are meticulous about setting clear and specific goals. They know what they want to achieve, and they prioritize their tasks accordingly. Goal-setting provides them with direction and motivation, guiding their actions toward success.

2. Morning Routines for a Strong Start:
Many high achievers swear by productive morning routines. These rituals include activities like exercise, meditation, journaling, and healthy breakfasts. Starting the day right helps them cultivate a positive mindset and energizes them for the challenges ahead.

3. Continuous Learning and Improvement:
High achievers are avid learners. They invest time in reading, attending seminars, and seeking mentors. This commitment to growth allows them to stay ahead in their fields and adapt to changing circumstances.

4. Effective Time Management:
Time management is a critical skill among high achievers. They use tools like calendars, to-do lists, and time-blocking to optimize their schedules. By allocating time wisely, they can focus on high-priority tasks.

5. Embracing Failure as a Learning Opportunity:
Rather than fearing failure, high achievers view it as a stepping stone to success. They learn from their mistakes, adjust their strategies, and persevere with unwavering determination.

6. Discipline and Consistency:
High achievers adhere to disciplined routines. They recognize that consistent effort is more valuable than sporadic bursts of activity. This consistency builds momentum and drives long-term success.

7. Networking and Building Relationships:

Building a strong network is crucial for high achievers. They understand the power of connections and actively cultivate relationships that can provide support, mentorship, and opportunities.

8. Mental and Physical Well-being:
Prioritizing health is a common trait among high achievers. They exercise regularly, eat nutritious diets, and practice mindfulness to maintain peak mental and physical performance.

9. Focus and Mindfulness:
High achievers excel in concentration. They minimize distractions, practice mindfulness, and stay present in the moment. This heightened focus enhances their productivity.

10. Resilience and Adaptability:
In the face of challenges, high achievers display remarkable resilience. They don't let setbacks deter them but instead use

adversity as a springboard for innovation and growth.

11. Celebrating Successes:
High achievers take time to celebrate their achievements, no matter how small. Recognizing success provides motivation and reinforces a positive mindset.

12. Giving Back and Contributing:
Many high achievers are passionate about giving back to their communities or supporting charitable causes. This sense of purpose drives them to perform at their best, knowing their success can make a difference.

High achievers are not superhuman; they are individuals who have honed specific habits, routines, and practices that consistently propel them toward excellence. By adopting some of these strategies and adapting them to your own life, you can unlock your potential and achieve remarkable success in your chosen endeavors. Remember that becoming a high achiever is a journey, and the path to sustained excellence is built one habit at a time.

Chapter 4

Overcoming Challenges

High achievers, those who consistently perform at their best, seem to possess a magic formula that eludes the rest of us. But the truth is, their success isn't a result of luck or innate talent alone. It's the product of deliberate habits, routines, and practices that foster excellence. In this article, we'll delve into the world of high achievers to uncover the secrets behind their consistent top performance.

1. Setting Clear Goals and Priorities:
High achievers are meticulous about setting clear and specific goals. They know what they want to achieve, and they prioritize their tasks accordingly. Goal-setting provides them with direction and motivation, guiding their actions toward success.

2. Morning Routines for a Strong Start:
Many high achievers swear by productive morning routines. These rituals include activities like exercise, meditation, journaling, and healthy breakfasts. Starting the day right helps them cultivate a positive mindset and energizes them for the challenges ahead.

3. Continuous Learning and Improvement:
High achievers are avid learners. They invest time in reading, attending seminars, and seeking mentors. This commitment to growth allows them to stay ahead in their fields and adapt to changing circumstances.

4. Effective Time Management:
Time management is a critical skill among high achievers. They use tools like calendars, to-do lists, and time-blocking to optimize their schedules. By allocating time wisely, they can focus on high-priority tasks.

5. Embracing Failure as a Learning Opportunity:
Rather than fearing failure, high achievers view it as a stepping stone to success. They learn from their mistakes, adjust their strategies, and persevere with unwavering determination.

6. Discipline and Consistency:
High achievers adhere to disciplined routines. They recognize that consistent effort is more valuable than sporadic bursts of activity. This consistency builds momentum and drives long-term success.

7. Networking and Building Relationships:
Building a strong network is crucial for high achievers. They understand the power of connections and actively cultivate relationships that can provide support, mentorship, and opportunities.

8. Mental and Physical Well-being:

Prioritizing health is a common trait among high achievers. They exercise regularly, eat nutritious diets, and practice mindfulness to maintain peak mental and physical performance.

9. Focus and Mindfulness:
High achievers excel in concentration. They minimize distractions, practice mindfulness, and stay present in the moment. This heightened focus enhances their productivity.

10. Resilience and Adaptability:
In the face of challenges, high achievers display remarkable resilience. They don't let setbacks deter them but instead use adversity as a springboard for innovation and growth.

11. Celebrating Successes:
High achievers take time to celebrate their achievements, no matter how small.

Recognizing success provides motivation and reinforces a positive mindset.

12. Giving Back and Contributing:
Many high achievers are passionate about giving back to their communities or supporting charitable causes. This sense of purpose drives them to perform at their best, knowing their success can make a difference.

High achievers are not superhuman; they are individuals who have honed specific habits, routines, and practices that consistently propel them toward excellence. By adopting some of these strategies and adapting them to your own life, you can unlock your potential and achieve remarkable success in your chosen endeavors. Remember that becoming a high achiever is a journey, and the path to sustained excellence is built one habit at a time.

Motivation and Inspiration

Motivation is the driving force that fuels our actions, goals, and aspirations. Whether you're striving for personal growth, pursuing a career, or embarking on a creative endeavor, understanding the sources of motivation and how to sustain it over the long term is crucial for success. Let's delve into the various sources of motivation and effective strategies to maintain it for the journey ahead.

Sources of Motivation:

1. Intrinsic Motivation: This comes from within. It's when you engage in an activity because you find it personally fulfilling or enjoyable. It's driven by a genuine interest or passion for the task itself.

2. Extrinsic Motivation: External factors, such as rewards, recognition, or praise, drive this type of motivation. It often plays a

role in achieving goals set by others or responding to external pressures.

3. Autonomy: Having control and autonomy over your decisions and actions can be a powerful motivator. When you feel in charge of your choices, you're more likely to stay motivated.

4. Purpose and Meaning: A clear sense of purpose and the belief that your actions contribute to something greater than yourself can be a strong source of motivation.

5. Mastery and Growth: The desire to improve, develop new skills, and achieve mastery in a particular area can be highly motivating. It's the satisfaction of making progress.

6. Social Connection: Human beings are inherently social creatures. Working with

others, receiving support, and feeling a sense of belonging can boost motivation.

7. Inspiration: Inspirational stories, role models, and experiences can spark motivation by showing what's possible and igniting a desire to achieve similar goals.

Strategies to Maintain Motivation for the Long Haul:

1. Set Clear Goals: Define your objectives with precision. Clear, well-defined goals provide direction and purpose.

2. Break Goals into Smaller Steps: Divide your goals into manageable, bite-sized tasks. This makes progress more tangible and achievable.

3. Celebrate Small Wins: Acknowledge and celebrate your achievements along the way. This boosts confidence and keeps you motivated.

4. Visualize Success: Imagine yourself accomplishing your goals. Visualization can reinforce your determination and desire to succeed.

5. Stay Accountable: Share your goals with a trusted friend, mentor, or coach. They can provide support and hold you accountable.

6. Maintain a Growth Mindset: Embrace challenges and view failures as opportunities to learn and grow. A growth mindset fosters resilience.

7. Stay Connected to Your "Why": Regularly remind yourself why you set your goals in the first place. Connecting to your deeper purpose rekindles motivation.

8. Create a Routine: Establish a daily or weekly routine that includes dedicated time for working on your goals. Consistency can prevent motivation from waning.

9. Seek Inspiration: Surround yourself with sources of inspiration, whether it's reading, attending seminars, or interacting with inspiring individuals.

10. Adapt and Adjust: Be flexible with your approach. If something isn't working, don't be afraid to pivot or try a different strategy.

11. Practice Self-Care: Taking care of your physical and mental well-being is essential for maintaining motivation over the long term. Ensure you get enough rest, exercise, and relaxation.

12. Stay Organized: Use tools like calendars, to-do lists, or project management apps to keep track of your goals and progress.

13. Review and Reflect: Periodically review your goals and assess your progress. Adjust your strategies as needed to stay on course.

In summary, motivation is a dynamic force that can come from various sources. To maintain it for the long haul, a combination of goal setting, self-awareness, perseverance, and adaptability is key. By understanding what motivates you and employing effective strategies, you can stay committed to your goals and achieve lasting success in your endeavors. Remember that motivation may ebb and flow, but with the right strategies, you can keep it burning brightly on your journey.

Chapter 5

Leadership and Influence

Leadership is not merely a title or position; it is a set of qualities that inspire, influence, and guide others towards a common goal. Effective leaders possess a unique blend of characteristics that set them apart. In this article, we will examine these qualities and explore why they are essential for leadership success.

1. Visionary:
Effective leaders have a clear and compelling vision for the future. They can see beyond the present and articulate a compelling picture of what could be. This vision serves as a guiding star, inspiring others to work towards a shared purpose.

2. Integrity:
Integrity is the foundation of trust. Leaders with integrity are honest, ethical, and

consistent in their actions and decisions. They adhere to a strong moral and ethical code, and their word is their bond.

3. Empathy:
Empathetic leaders understand and connect with the emotions and experiences of others. They listen actively, show genuine concern for their team members, and foster a sense of belonging and support.

4. Effective Communication:
Leaders must be effective communicators. They can convey their ideas clearly and inspire others with their words. They listen actively, ask questions, and provide feedback to foster open and transparent communication.

5. Adaptability:
The world is constantly changing, and effective leaders must be adaptable. They embrace change, navigate uncertainty with

composure, and lead their teams through transitions with flexibility and resilience.

6. Decisiveness:
Leaders are often faced with tough decisions. Effective leaders have the ability to make timely and informed choices, even in challenging situations. They weigh options carefully and take calculated risks when necessary.

7. Confidence:
Confidence is contagious. Leaders who believe in themselves and their abilities inspire confidence in others. They exude a sense of self-assuredness that encourages team members to follow their lead.

8. Accountability:
Accountable leaders take responsibility for their actions and outcomes. They do not shy away from owning up to mistakes but use them as learning opportunities. They set a

high standard of accountability for themselves and their teams.

9. Delegation:
Leaders understand that they cannot do everything alone. They delegate tasks and responsibilities effectively, trusting their team members to carry out their roles competently. Delegation allows leaders to focus on strategic priorities.

10. Empowerment:
Effective leaders empower their team members. They provide the necessary resources, support, and autonomy for individuals to excel in their roles. Empowerment fosters a sense of ownership and responsibility.

11. Resilience:
Leadership can be demanding and stressful. Resilient leaders bounce back from setbacks and maintain their composure during

challenging times. They inspire confidence and a sense of stability.

12. Inspiring Others:
Effective leaders have the ability to inspire and motivate their team members. They lead by example, set high standards, and instill a sense of purpose and enthusiasm in their followers.

13. Continuous Learning:
Leadership is a journey of growth. Effective leaders are lifelong learners. They seek out opportunities to expand their knowledge, skills, and perspectives.

Effective leadership is a dynamic and multifaceted quality that combines vision, integrity, empathy, communication, adaptability, and more. Leaders who possess these qualities inspire trust, promote collaboration, and drive their teams towards success. While these traits may come naturally to some, they can also be developed and honed over time through self-awareness and deliberate practice. In a rapidly changing world, effective leadership remains a critical force for positive change and progress in organizations and communities alike.

The Art of Leadership: Inspiring and Influencing Positively

Effective leadership goes beyond managing tasks and making decisions. It involves inspiring and positively influencing others to achieve common goals. Great leaders have the ability to motivate and empower their teams, fostering a collaborative environment where everyone can thrive. In this article, we will explore the key ways in which effective leaders can inspire and influence others positively.

1. Lead by Example:
One of the most powerful ways to inspire others is to lead by example. When a leader

sets high standards for themselves, demonstrates integrity, and exhibits a strong work ethic, it sends a clear message to the team. Your actions speak louder than words, and others are more likely to follow suit when they see you living the values you espouse.

2. Communicate with Clarity and Transparency:
Effective communication is a cornerstone of positive leadership. Leaders should communicate their vision, goals, and expectations clearly and consistently. Being transparent about challenges, successes, and setbacks builds trust within the team. Open communication encourages collaboration and helps everyone understand their role in achieving shared objectives.

3. Empower and Delegate:
A strong leader knows how to delegate effectively. Empowering team members by entrusting them with responsibilities not

only shows confidence in their abilities but also allows them to grow and develop. Delegation distributes the workload, fosters a sense of ownership, and can lead to innovative solutions.

4. Provide Support and Guidance:
Effective leaders are not just supervisors; they are mentors and coaches. They offer support, guidance, and constructive feedback to help team members reach their full potential. Recognizing and nurturing individual strengths and addressing weaknesses in a positive way contributes to personal and team growth.

5. Create a Positive Work Environment:
Leaders play a significant role in shaping the work environment. A positive, inclusive, and respectful workplace culture encourages team members to thrive. Acknowledging and celebrating achievements, no matter how small, boosts morale and motivates the team.

6. Foster Innovation and Creativity:
Inspiring leaders encourage innovative thinking and creativity. They provide space for team members to brainstorm, experiment, and take calculated risks. Encouraging fresh ideas and solutions can lead to breakthroughs and keep the team engaged.

7. Embrace Diversity and Inclusion:
In today's diverse world, effective leaders recognize the value of diversity and inclusion. They create an environment where everyone's perspectives and backgrounds are respected and valued. This fosters creativity, innovation, and a sense of belonging.

8. Lead with Empathy and Emotional Intelligence:
Empathy is a hallmark of positive leadership. Understanding and empathizing with team members' emotions and

challenges builds strong connections. Leaders with high emotional intelligence can adapt their communication and leadership style to suit the needs of their team.

9. Set Clear Goals and Celebrate Achievements:
A leader's role includes setting clear, achievable goals and milestones. Celebrating achievements, no matter how small, reinforces a sense of accomplishment and motivates team members to continue striving for success.

10. Continuously Learn and Grow:
Effective leaders are lifelong learners. They stay current in their field, seek feedback, and are open to personal and professional growth. This commitment to self-improvement sets a positive example for the team and demonstrates a dedication to excellence.

Effective leadership is about more than just managing people; it's about inspiring and positively influencing others to reach their potential. By leading by example, communicating effectively, empowering, and fostering a supportive environment, leaders can create a workplace where individuals are motivated to excel. Great leaders understand that their success is intertwined with the success of their team and work tirelessly to ensure that everyone can thrive and achieve their best. In doing so, they leave a lasting, positive impact on their organizations and the individuals they lead.

Chapter 6

Creativity and Innovation

Creativity and innovative thinking are not limited to artists and inventors; they are vital skills that can enrich various aspects of our lives. From problem-solving in our careers to spicing up our daily routines, fostering creativity and innovation can lead to a more fulfilling and dynamic existence. In this article, we will explore techniques to nurture these essential skills across different dimensions of life.

1. Embrace Curiosity:
Curiosity is the spark that ignites creativity. Cultivate a curious mindset by asking questions, exploring new subjects, and seeking out diverse experiences. Curiosity is the fuel for innovative thinking, encouraging you to see the world through different lenses.

2. Step Out of Your Comfort Zone:
Innovation often happens when we step beyond the familiar. Challenge yourself to try new activities, visit new places, or connect with people from different backgrounds. Comfort zones may feel cozy, but they rarely foster creative breakthroughs.

3. Creative Daily Practices:
Incorporate creative routines into your daily life. Whether it's journaling, drawing, or brainstorming, setting aside dedicated time for creativity can yield inventive ideas and solutions.

4. Collaborate and Network:
Creative sparks can fly when you collaborate with others. Engage in brainstorming sessions, seek out diverse perspectives, and participate in creative communities. Networking can lead to fresh insights and opportunities for innovation.

5. Embrace Failure:
Fear of failure can stifle creativity. Embrace failure as a learning opportunity. When you remove the fear of making mistakes, you open the door to experimentation and new ideas.

6. Mindfulness and Meditation:
Mindfulness practices can enhance creativity by helping you focus on the present moment and quieting your inner critic. Meditation can clear mental clutter and create space for innovative thinking.

7. Read Widely:
Expose yourself to a variety of genres and subjects through reading. Literature, non-fiction, and even fiction can provide new perspectives and ideas that stimulate creativity.

8. Problem-Solving Exercises:
Engage in problem-solving exercises or puzzles regularly. These activities sharpen

your analytical thinking and encourage creative problem-solving.

9. Break Routine:
Introduce spontaneity into your life. Break from routine, take a different route to work, or change your daily rituals. Unpredictability can lead to fresh perspectives and innovative solutions.

10. Continuous Learning:
Embrace lifelong learning. Explore online courses, attend workshops, and enroll in classes that interest you. Continuous learning broadens your knowledge base, sparking new ideas.

11. Playfulness and Imagination:
Allow your inner child to emerge. Engage in playful activities, daydream, and let your imagination run wild. Playfulness fosters creativity and reminds you that innovation can be fun.

12. Document Ideas:
Keep a notebook or digital journal to jot down ideas and inspirations as they come to you. This habit ensures you don't forget potentially groundbreaking thoughts.

13. Emulate Innovators:
Study the lives and methodologies of innovators in your field of interest. Understand their creative processes and draw inspiration from their journeys.

14. Seek Feedback:
Share your ideas and creations with others, and be open to feedback. Constructive criticism can help refine your concepts and lead to innovative improvements.

15. Reflect and Iterate:
Periodically reflect on your creative journey. What worked? What didn't? Use these insights to iterate and refine your approach to fostering creativity.

Creativity and innovative thinking are not reserved for the elite; they are skills that can be cultivated and applied to enrich every facet of our lives. By embracing curiosity, stepping out of comfort zones, and incorporating daily creative practices, you can unlock a world of fresh ideas and solutions. Remember, creativity is a lifelong journey, and the more you nurture it, the more it can transform and elevate various aspects of your life, from your career to your daily routines, and even your personal growth. Start today, and watch as creativity and innovation flourish in your world.

Positive Psychology

Happiness and well-being are universal human desires. People across cultures and ages have sought to unravel the mysteries of leading a fulfilling life. Fortunately, in recent decades, scicncc has made significant strides in understanding the intricacies of happiness and well-being. In this article, we will explore the science behind happiness and well-being, shedding light on the factors that contribute to our sense of contentment and purpose.

Defining Happiness and Well-Being: Happiness and well-being are multifaceted concepts that encompass various dimensions of our lives. They are not merely the absence of suffering but the presence of positive emotions, life satisfaction, and a sense of purpose. Researchers often break down well-being into two main components:

1. Hedonic Well-Being: This aspect of well-being focuses on the pursuit of pleasure and the avoidance of pain. It includes positive emotions like joy, gratitude, and contentment, and it seeks to maximize life satisfaction.

2. Eudaimonic Well-Being: Eudaimonic well-being emphasizes the pursuit of meaning and purpose in life. It involves

self-realization, personal growth, and the realization of one's full potential.

The Science of Happiness:
Researchers in fields such as psychology, neuroscience, and positive psychology have explored the science of happiness and well-being in depth. Here are some key findings:

1. The Role of Genetics: Studies suggest that about 50% of our happiness is determined by our genetics. Some people may have a genetic predisposition to be happier than others, but this doesn't mean that happiness is fixed.

2. The Impact of Circumstances: External circumstances, such as income, health, and social relationships, have a limited impact on our long-term happiness. Once basic needs are met, additional wealth or possessions do not significantly increase happiness.

3. The Power of Relationships: Social connections are one of the most robust predictors of happiness and well-being. Maintaining strong, positive relationships with friends and family contributes significantly to life satisfaction.

4. Positive Emotions: Experiencing positive emotions, like gratitude, kindness, and love, not only enhance hedonic well-being but also promote physical health and resilience.

5. Mindfulness and Flow: Practices such as mindfulness meditation and engaging in activities that induce a state of "flow" can lead to increased eudaimonic well-being by fostering a sense of presence, purpose, and personal growth.

6. Meaningful Goals: Pursuing meaningful goals and engaging in activities aligned with our values can enhance well-being.

Goal-setting and achievement provide a sense of purpose and accomplishment.

7. The Role of Resilience: Resilience—the ability to bounce back from adversity—is closely linked to well-being. Developing resilience through challenges can ultimately lead to greater happiness.

8. Gratitude and Positive Psychology: The field of positive psychology has explored interventions like gratitude journaling, which have been shown to boost well-being by focusing on positive aspects of life.

9. The Impact of Acts of Kindness: Engaging in acts of kindness and prosocial behavior not only benefits others but also enhances one's own happiness and well-being.

10. The Brain and Happiness: Neuroscientists have identified brain regions associated with happiness, such as the prefrontal cortex. These regions play a

role in regulating emotions and maintaining positive well-being.

The science of happiness and well-being paints a comprehensive picture of what contributes to a fulfilling life. It underscores that happiness is not a fleeting emotion but a state that can be nurtured and cultivated through various practices and perspectives. While our genetics and external circumstances play a role, the choices we make, the relationships we foster, and the mindset we cultivate are equally—if not more—crucial in shaping our well-being. By understanding the science behind happiness, we can embark on a journey to lead more satisfying, purposeful lives and help others do the same. Remember, happiness is not a destination; it's a lifelong journey.

The Psychology Behind a Fulfilling Life: Unlocking the Secrets of Well-Being

The pursuit of a fulfilling life is a universal aspiration. What does it take to experience lasting happiness, contentment, and a sense of purpose? The answer lies in the field of positive psychology, which delves into the psychological aspects of well-being. In this article, we will explore the psychology behind a fulfilling life and uncover the key principles that can help us lead richer and more satisfying lives.

1. Positive Emotions: The Foundation of Well-Being:
Positive emotions play a central role in a fulfilling life. Research in positive psychology highlights the importance of cultivating emotions like gratitude, joy, and compassion. Emotions not only enhance our daily experiences but also contribute to our overall sense of well-being.

2. Engagement: The Flow State:

Being fully engaged in activities that challenge and inspire us is a crucial component of a fulfilling life. Psychologist Mihaly Csikszentmihalyi coined the term "flow" to describe this state of complete absorption and focus. Engaging activities provide a sense of accomplishment and fulfillment.

3. Meaning and Purpose: A Driving Force:
A sense of meaning and purpose is a cornerstone of well-being. Individuals who have a clear sense of their values and life goals tend to report higher life satisfaction. Identifying your purpose and aligning your actions with it can provide a profound sense of fulfillment.

4. Positive Relationships: The Power of Connection:
Positive psychology underscores the significance of nurturing meaningful relationships. Quality connections with family, friends, and the community

contribute significantly to happiness and well-being. Building and maintaining strong social bonds is essential.

5. Accomplishment and Achievement:
Setting and achieving meaningful goals provide a sense of accomplishment and satisfaction. Whether they are related to your career, personal development, or hobbies, reaching milestones can boost self-esteem and contribute to a fulfilling life.

6. Resilience and Coping Skills:
Resilience, the ability to bounce back from adversity, is another crucial psychological factor. Resilient individuals can navigate life's challenges with grace and emerge from difficult situations with increased strength and wisdom.

7. Mindfulness and Well-Being:
Mindfulness practices, such as meditation and mindfulness-based stress reduction, have gained recognition for their positive

impact on well-being. These practices promote self-awareness, reduce stress, and enhance overall mental health.

8. Gratitude: The Attitude of Abundance:
Cultivating gratitude is a simple yet powerful psychological tool for enhancing well-being. Keeping a gratitude journal or regularly reflecting on the things you're thankful for can shift your focus toward positivity and contentment.

9. Acts of Kindness and Altruism:
Performing acts of kindness and altruism not only benefit others but also boost your own well-being. Helping others and contributing to the greater good can create a profound sense of fulfillment and purpose.

10. Self-Care and Well-Being Practices:
Taking care of your physical and mental health is fundamental. Regular exercise, adequate sleep, a balanced diet, and stress

management techniques are all vital for well-being.

11. Personal Growth and Continuous Learning:

A commitment to personal growth and lifelong learning can lead to increased life satisfaction. Expanding your knowledge, skills, and experiences can provide a sense of achievement and fulfillment.

12. Positive Self-Image:

A healthy self-image is crucial for well-being. Practicing self-compassion, embracing imperfections, and nurturing self-esteem contribute to a positive self-concept.

13. Goal Alignment with Values:

Ensure your goals align with your core values. When your actions are in harmony with your values, you experience a deeper sense of purpose and fulfillment.

The psychology behind a fulfilling life is a multifaceted and evolving field. It highlights the importance of positive emotions, engagement, meaning, and positive relationships in our pursuit of happiness. By incorporating these principles into our daily lives and nurturing our psychological well-being, we can unlock the secrets to a richer, more satisfying existence. The journey to a fulfilling life begins with self-awareness, mindfulness, and a commitment to personal growth. Ultimately, understanding the psychology of well-being empowers us to lead happier, more fulfilling lives, not just for ourselves but also for those around us.

Chapter 7

Personal Growth and Transformation

Personal growth is a lifelong journey of self-discovery, self-improvement, and the pursuit of one's full potential. It involves developing skills, expanding knowledge, nurturing emotional well-being, and evolving as an individual. Here are insights and practical advice to help you embark on and sustain your personal growth journey:

1. Self-Awareness: The Foundation of Growth:
   - Insight: Self-awareness is the key to personal growth. It involves understanding your strengths, weaknesses, values, beliefs, and emotional triggers.
   - Practical Advice: Dedicate time to introspection. Journaling, meditation, and seeking feedback from others can help you gain insight into yourself.

2. Set Meaningful Goals:

   - Insight: Goals provide direction and purpose in life. Meaningful goals align with your values and passions.

   - Practical Advice: Define clear and specific goals. Break them into smaller, manageable steps, and regularly review your progress.

3. Embrace Continuous Learning:

   - Insight: Lifelong learning is essential for personal growth. It keeps your mind open to new ideas and possibilities.

   - Practical Advice: Read widely, take courses, attend workshops, and seek out experiences that challenge and expand your knowledge.

4. Cultivate Resilience:

   - Insight: Resilience is the ability to bounce back from setbacks. It's a valuable trait for personal growth.

   - Practical Advice: Embrace challenges as opportunities for growth. Develop coping strategies, practice self-compassion, and learn from failures.

5. Develop Emotional Intelligence:
   - Insight: Emotional intelligence involves recognizing, understanding, and managing your own emotions and those of others.
   - Practical Advice: Practice active listening, empathy, and effective communication. Regularly check in with your emotions and seek emotional balance.

6. Embrace Change:
   - Insight: Personal growth often involves stepping out of your comfort zone and embracing change.
   - Practical Advice: Embrace uncertainty, take calculated risks, and view change as an opportunity for learning and growth.

7. Build Healthy Habits:
   - Insight: Habits shape your daily life. Healthy habits contribute to personal growth and well-being.

- Practical Advice: Identify habits that support your goals and work on them consistently. Replace unhealthy habits with positive ones.

8. Seek Feedback and Guidance:
   - Insight: Feedback from others can provide valuable insights and perspectives on your growth journey.
   - Practical Advice: Be open to feedback and seek mentorship or coaching when needed. Constructive criticism is a path to improvement.

9. Maintain a Growth Mindset:
   - Insight: A growth mindset is the belief that abilities and intelligence can be developed through effort and learning.
   - Practical Advice: Challenge fixed beliefs about your limitations. Embrace challenges, persevere through setbacks, and see failures as opportunities to learn.

10. Prioritize Self-Care:

- Insight: Taking care of your physical and mental well-being is crucial for personal growth.

- Practical Advice: Make time for self-care activities like exercise, meditation, adequate sleep, and stress management. Nourish your body and mind.

11. Practice Gratitude:

- Insight: Gratitude cultivates a positive outlook and enhances personal growth.

- Practical Advice: Regularly express gratitude for the people, experiences, and opportunities in your life. Keep a gratitude journal if it helps.

12. Reflect and Adjust:

- Insight: Personal growth is an ongoing process. Periodic reflection and adjustment are necessary.

- Practical Advice: Set aside time to reflect on your progress, reassess your goals, and make necessary adjustments to your path.

In conclusion, personal growth is a transformative journey that requires self-awareness, continuous learning, resilience, and a commitment to improvement. By embracing these insights and following practical advice, you can unlock your full potential, cultivate a fulfilling life, and make a positive impact on both yourself and those around you. Remember that personal growth is not a destination; it's a lifelong adventure.

Unleash Your Potential: A Guide to Personal Transformation

Personal transformation is a profound journey toward becoming the best version of oneself. It's a process of self-discovery, growth, and self-improvement that can lead to a more fulfilling and purposeful life. In this guide, we will explore insights and offer practical advice to help you embark on your personal transformation journey.

1. Self-Awareness: The Starting Point:
The foundation of personal transformation is self-awareness. Begin by reflecting on your strengths, weaknesses, values, and aspirations. Understand your motivations and fears. Self-awareness is the mirror that reveals who you truly are.

2. Set Clear Goals and Intentions:
Identify what you want to achieve in your personal transformation journey. These goals can range from improving your physical health to developing new skills or finding greater meaning in your life. Setting clear intentions provides direction.

3. Embrace Change and Growth:
Personal transformation requires change and growth. Embrace the discomfort that often accompanies change, as it signifies you are expanding beyond your comfort zone. Be open to learning from your experiences.

4. Self-Care Is Non-Negotiable:

Take care of your physical, emotional, and mental well-being. Prioritize exercise, nutrition, sleep, and stress management. A healthy body and mind provide the foundation for personal growth.

5. Cultivate a Growth Mindset:
Adopt a growth mindset, believing that your abilities and intelligence can be developed through effort and learning. Embrace challenges and view failures as opportunities for growth.

6. Face Your Fears:
Personal transformation often involves confronting your fears and limiting beliefs. Challenge the thoughts that hold you back, and take calculated risks. Growth happens when you step outside your comfort zone.

7. Develop Resilience:
Resilience is the ability to bounce back from adversity. Strengthen your resilience by building a support system, practicing

mindfulness, and maintaining a positive outlook.

8. Continuous Learning and Skill Development:
Engage in lifelong learning. Acquire new skills, pursue hobbies, and expand your knowledge. Learning not only keeps your mind sharp but also opens up new opportunities for personal growth.

9. Practice Gratitude:
Cultivate gratitude as a daily practice. Reflect on the positive aspects of your life, both big and small. Gratitude shifts your focus toward abundance and enhances your overall well-being.

10. Seek Inspiration and Role Models:
Surround yourself with inspiring individuals and role models who embody the qualities you aspire to have. Learn from their experiences and seek guidance when needed.

11. Build Meaningful Relationships:
Nurture meaningful relationships with friends, family, and mentors. These connections provide support, guidance, and a sense of belonging, which are essential for personal transformation.

12. Accept Imperfection:
Perfection is an unattainable ideal. Embrace imperfection and learn from your mistakes. Understand that your journey toward becoming the best version of yourself is a continuous process.

13. Mindfulness and Reflection:
Practice mindfulness to stay present and self-reflect regularly. It helps you gain insights into your thoughts, emotions, and behaviors, allowing for intentional personal growth.

14. Consistency and Patience:

Personal transformation takes time and consistency. Be patient with yourself, and stay committed to your goals even when progress seems slow.

15. Celebrate Progress:
Acknowledge and celebrate your achievements and milestones along the way. Recognizing your progress boosts motivation and reinforces positive behaviors.

Personal transformation is a lifelong journey that involves self-awareness, growth, and self-improvement. By incorporating these insights and practical advice into your life, you can embark on a path to becoming the best version of yourself. Remember that personal transformation is not a destination but a continuous process of evolution and self-discovery. Embrace the journey, and you will unlock your true potential and live a more meaningful and fulfilling life.

Chapter 8

Purpose and Meaning

In the pursuit of happiness and fulfillment, many individuals seek a deeper sense of purpose. This desire for meaning in life goes beyond mere existence; it's about understanding why we do what we do and finding significance in our actions. In this article, we will delve into the significance of living a purpose-driven life and the profound impact it can have on our overall well-being.

1. What Is a Purpose-Driven Life?:
A purpose-driven life is one in which individuals have a clear sense of their values, passions, and overarching goals. It's a life guided by a deep sense of purpose that directs their actions and choices.

2. The Significance of Purpose:

a. Motivation and Direction: Having a purpose provides motivation and direction. It answers the fundamental question, "Why am I doing this?" This clarity can drive you to take meaningful actions and achieve your goals.

b. Resilience: Purpose serves as a source of resilience during difficult times. When faced with challenges, individuals with a strong sense of purpose are more likely to persevere, as they see setbacks as part of their larger journey.

c. Improved Well-Being: Studies have shown that individuals who live purpose-driven lives report higher levels of life satisfaction and overall well-being. They tend to experience lower levels of stress and are more resilient to mental health issues.

d. Enhanced Relationships: Purpose can also enhance relationships. When individuals align their values and goals with their partners, friends, or communities, it fosters a sense of connection and mutual understanding.

3. Finding Meaning in Actions:
a. Pursuit of Passions: Identifying your passions is a crucial step in living a purpose-driven life. What activities or causes make you feel most alive? Pursuing these passions can infuse your actions with meaning.

b. Helping Others: Acts of kindness and altruism often bring deep meaning to one's life. Whether through volunteering, supporting friends and family, or contributing to a greater cause, helping others creates a profound sense of purpose.

c. Personal Growth: Personal development and continuous learning can be intrinsically rewarding. As you grow and evolve, you find meaning in your progress and the journey itself.

d. Aligning with Values: Living in alignment with your core values is at the heart of a purpose-driven life. When your actions reflect what you hold dear, you experience a sense of integrity and authenticity.

e. Making a Difference: Many individuals find meaning by making a positive impact on the world, whether through their work, advocacy, or creative endeavors. Knowing that your actions contribute to something larger can be deeply fulfilling.

4. Practical Steps to Living a Purpose-Driven Life:
a. Self-Reflection: Start by reflecting on your values, interests, and passions. Consider what activities make you lose track of time and bring you joy.

b. Set Clear Goals: Define specific goals that align with your purpose. These goals can serve as milestones on your journey toward a purpose-driven life.

c. Take Action: Purpose requires action. Act on your passions and values, whether it's through your career, personal projects, or relationships.

d. Seek Connection: Connect with like-minded individuals who share your values and interests. Join communities, organizations, or support networks that align with your purpose.

e. Embrace Challenges: Challenges are part of the journey. Embrace them as opportunities for growth and learning. Overcoming obstacles can deepen your sense of purpose.

Living a purpose-driven life is about infusing your actions with meaning and aligning your values with your choices. It's a journey of self-discovery, personal growth, and contribution to something greater than yourself. Finding purpose not only enhances your well-being but also empowers you to make a positive impact on the world. As you embark on this journey, remember that your sense of purpose can evolve and change over time, so stay open to new possibilities and opportunities for growth. In the end, living a purpose-driven life can lead to a deeply fulfilling and meaningful existence.

Health and Wellness

Unlocking one's potential and achieving greatness is a multifaceted journey that encompasses not only ambition and skill but also the profound connection between physical and mental health. These two aspects of well-being are not separate entities; they work in tandem to propel individuals toward their highest potential. In this article, we will explore the crucial role of physical and mental health in unlocking greatness.

Physical Health: The Foundation of Greatness

1. Energy and Vitality: Physical health is the bedrock upon which greatness is built. When you prioritize your physical well-being through regular exercise, balanced nutrition, and sufficient rest, you boost your energy levels and vitality. This newfound vigor becomes the fuel that powers your ambitions and pursuits.

2. Resilience: Physical health contributes to resilience. A healthy body is better equipped to withstand stress and adversity. When you're physically well, you can bounce back from setbacks more effectively, keeping you on the path toward greatness.

3. Mental Clarity: Physical fitness enhances mental clarity. Regular exercise improves cognitive function, increases focus, and sharpens problem-solving skills. A clear

mind is essential for making informed decisions and pursuing ambitious goals.

4. Confidence and Self-Esteem: Achieving physical fitness goals can boost confidence and self-esteem. When you feel good about your body and health, you carry that positivity into other areas of your life, fostering a mindset of greatness.

Mental Health: The Catalyst for Greatness

1. Emotional Resilience: Mental health is the guardian of emotional resilience. It equips you with the tools to manage stress, anxiety, and emotional challenges. With a resilient mind, you can face adversity head-on and maintain your focus on long-term goals.

2. Creativity and Innovation: A healthy mind fosters creativity and innovation. Mental well-being encourages out-of-the-box thinking, problem-solving, and the generation of groundbreaking ideas.

It's the breeding ground for greatness in any field.

3. Positive Mindset: Mental health cultivates a positive mindset. Optimism and a belief in your abilities are key ingredients for achieving greatness. A healthy mind enables you to maintain a can-do attitude even in the face of daunting challenges.

4. Relationships and Networking: Mental health plays a significant role in building and maintaining meaningful relationships. Strong connections with others can open doors to opportunities, collaborations, and mentorships that propel you toward greatness.

The Symbiotic Relationship:
Physical and mental health do not exist in isolation; they interact and amplify each other's effects. A strong body supports a resilient mind, while a positive mental outlook can motivate you to take care of

your physical well-being. The symbiotic relationship between these two aspects creates a harmonious environment for unlocking your potential and achieving greatness.

Practical Steps to Prioritize Physical and Mental Health for Greatness

1. Regular Exercise: Incorporate physical activity into your routine. Aim for a mix of cardio, strength training, and flexibility exercises to keep your body in peak condition.

2. Balanced Nutrition: Fuel your body with a balanced diet rich in nutrients. Proper nutrition provides the energy needed for both physical and mental tasks.

3. Adequate Rest: Prioritize sleep. Quality rest is essential for physical recovery and mental rejuvenation.

4. Mindfulness and Meditation: Practice mindfulness and meditation to enhance mental clarity, reduce stress, and foster emotional resilience.

5. Seek Professional Help: If you face mental health challenges, seek support from a mental health professional. Therapy and counseling can provide valuable tools for maintaining a healthy mind.

6. Set Realistic Goals: Establish realistic goals for both physical fitness and mental well-being. Achievable milestones provide a sense of accomplishment and motivation.

7. Social Connections: Foster meaningful relationships with friends, family, and mentors. A support system can be invaluable in times of need.

Greatness is not a distant aspiration; it is a journey that begins with the recognition of the profound connection between physical and mental health. By prioritizing your well-being in both these areas, you create the ideal environment for unlocking your potential and achieving greatness. Remember, greatness is not solely defined by external achievements but also by the growth, fulfillment, and positive impact you bring to your life and the lives of others. Prioritize your physical and mental health, and you will be well on your way to a life of significance and accomplishment.

Chapter 9

Success Stories

Here are a few inspiring stories of individuals who have tapped into their unseen potential and achieved remarkable feats:

1: Sarah's Journey to Leadership

My name is Sarah, and I'd like to share my story of personal transformation. A few years ago, I was stuck in a dead-end job with little self-confidence. Then, one day, I attended a leadership seminar, and it changed my life. I realized I had untapped leadership potential. I began taking on more responsibilities at work and mentoring colleagues. Fast forward to today, I'm now a respected team leader, and I'm pursuing an MBA to further develop my skills. I never thought I could achieve this level of success, but tapping into my unseen potential changed everything.

2: David's Marathon Victory

Hi, I'm David, and I'd like to tell you about my journey from an average runner to a marathon champion. I always enjoyed running, but I never considered myself an athlete. One day, a friend encouraged me to train for a marathon. I took the challenge, and it was grueling. But I tapped into my hidden reserves of determination and resilience. After months of hard work, I not only finished the marathon but won first place in my age group. It showed me that I had untapped potential for athleticism I never knew existed.

3: Maria's Entrepreneurial Triumph

My name is Maria, and I want to share how I went from being a stay-at-home mom to a successful entrepreneur. I always had a passion for crafting, but I never thought it could become a business. However, during a challenging time in my life, I decided to turn my hobby into a small venture. I worked tirelessly, tapping into my creativity and determination. Today, my crafting business is thriving, and I've discovered a depth of entrepreneurial potential I never knew I had.

4: John's Journey to Becoming a Published Author

I'm John, and I want to share my story of becoming a published author. For years, I worked in a corporate job, feeling unfulfilled. I had always loved writing but never pursued it seriously. One day, I decided to write a novel in my spare time. It was a slow process, but I tapped into my passion for storytelling. After countless revisions and rejections, my first book was published. Now, I'm a full-time author, and my novels have touched the lives of many readers. I discovered my hidden potential as a writer, and it's changed my life.

These stories highlight the transformative power of tapping into unseen potential. Each individual found their unique strengths and abilities, proving that remarkable feats are within reach when we believe in ourselves and harness our untapped potential.

Chapter 10

Time Management and Productivity

Effective time management and productivity strategies can significantly increase your accomplishments and help you make the most of your day. Here are some practical strategies to help you manage your time efficiently and boost productivity:

1. Prioritize Tasks:

- Identify your most important tasks (MITs) for the day and tackle them first. Prioritizing ensures that you address critical items before less important ones.

2. Set Clear Goals:

- Establish specific, measurable, achievable, relevant, and time-bound (SMART) goals. Having clear objectives helps you stay focused and track your progress.

3. Create a To-Do List:
   - Use a to-do list or task management app to organize your daily and weekly tasks. Update your list regularly to stay on top of your responsibilities.

4. Time Blocking:
   - Allocate specific blocks of time for different tasks or types of work. This approach helps you concentrate on one task at a time and minimizes distractions.

5. Eliminate Distractions:
   - Identify common distractions in your work environment, such as social media or noisy coworkers, and take steps to minimize or eliminate them during focused work periods.

6. Use the Pomodoro Technique:
   - Work in focused intervals, typically 25 minutes, followed by a 5-minute break. After completing four cycles, take a longer

break. This technique can boost concentration and productivity.

7. Learn to Say No:

- Avoid overcommitting yourself. Politely decline tasks or projects that don't align with your priorities or that you don't have the capacity to handle.

8. Delegate Tasks:

- If possible, delegate tasks to team members or colleagues. Delegation frees up your time for more critical responsibilities and empowers others.

9. Batch Similar Tasks:

- Group similar tasks together and tackle them in one go. For example, answer emails, make phone calls, or complete administrative work in dedicated time blocks.

10. Use Technology Wisely:

- Leverage productivity apps and tools to streamline tasks. Calendar apps, project management software, and note-taking apps can help you stay organized.

11. Limit Multitasking:
- While multitasking might seem efficient, it can lead to decreased productivity and increased errors. Focus on one task at a time for better results.

12. Take Regular Breaks:
- Short breaks during work can boost productivity and prevent burnout. Use breaks to stretch, walk, or clear your mind.

13. Review and Reflect:
- Regularly assess your progress and make adjustments to your time management strategies. Learn from what works and what doesn't.

14. Set Boundaries:

- Establish clear boundaries between work and personal life. This separation helps maintain work-life balance and prevents burnout.

15. Continuous Learning:
    - Invest time in learning about time management and productivity techniques. New strategies and tools are continually emerging.

16. Get Adequate Sleep and Exercise:
    - A well-rested and physically active body and mind are more productive. Prioritize sleep and exercise to maintain your energy levels.

Remember that effective time management is a skill that takes time to develop. Experiment with these strategies to find what works best for you, and be patient with yourself as you implement changes to your routine. Over time, you'll find that these strategies can help you maximize your accomplishments and achieve your goals more efficiently.

Communication and Relationships

Communication and relationships are the cornerstones of personal and professional development. These two interlinked elements not only enrich our lives but also propel us toward growth, success, and fulfillment. In this exploration, we will delve into how effective communication and building positive relationships contribute to personal and professional growth.

1.   Effective Communication Fosters Understanding:
Effective communication is a two-way street that involves not just talking but also listening. When we communicate effectively, we ensure that our thoughts, ideas, and intentions are understood. This understanding is the foundation of personal growth because it allows us to share

knowledge, learn from others, and gain valuable insights.

2.   Communication   Enhances Problem-Solving Skills:
Effective communication is a vital tool for problem-solving. When individuals openly share their perspectives and collaborate, they can address challenges more efficiently. This problem-solving approach not only resolves immediate issues but also cultivates critical thinking and adaptability, fostering personal and professional growth.

3.   Positive   Relationships   Inspire Confidence:
Positive relationships are built on trust, respect, and open communication. These elements create an environment where individuals feel secure and valued. Such relationships inspire confidence, allowing us to take calculated risks, explore new opportunities, and strive for personal and

professional growth without the fear of failure.

4. Feedback and Self-Improvement:
Effective communication includes giving and receiving feedback constructively. Constructive feedback helps individuals identify areas for improvement and offers guidance on how to enhance their skills and abilities. This feedback loop is essential for continuous self-improvement, a key aspect of personal growth.

5. Networking Opens Doors:
Building positive relationships through networking can significantly impact professional growth. Connections with colleagues, mentors, and industry peers can lead to new opportunities, collaborations, and career advancement. These relationships create a supportive network that can propel individuals to higher levels of success.

6. Conflict Resolution and Emotional Intelligence:

Effective communication is crucial in resolving conflicts, a skill highly valued in both personal and professional spheres. Constructive conflict resolution relies on emotional intelligence, which involves recognizing and managing emotions in ourselves and others. Developing emotional intelligence through effective communication contributes to personal growth by fostering empathy and interpersonal skills.

7. Building a Support System:

Positive relationships provide a vital support system during challenging times. Whether it's personal setbacks or professional obstacles, having a network of supportive individuals can offer encouragement, guidance, and perspective. This support system boosts resilience and aids in overcoming setbacks, contributing to personal growth.

8. Encouraging Lifelong Learning:
Engaging in open, constructive conversations with others often leads to learning opportunities. Exposure to diverse perspectives and knowledge broadens our horizons and encourages lifelong learning. This thirst for knowledge is a driving force behind personal and professional growth.

9. Enhancing Leadership Skills:
Positive relationships and effective communication are at the heart of leadership. Leaders who excel in these areas inspire, motivate, and guide their teams to success. Developing leadership skills through effective communication and relationship-building can lead to professional growth and career advancement.

In conclusion, effective communication and building positive relationships are dynamic forces that drive personal and professional growth. These skills not only enhance understanding, problem-solving, and self-improvement but also inspire confidence, open doors to opportunities, and provide crucial support systems. By nurturing these essential elements, individuals can unlock their full potential and thrive in both their personal and professional lives.